T0358138

PUT DOWN AT BIRTH

Growing up on the Right Side of the Tracks on Sydney's North Shore

By

Sandra J. Darroch

ISBN 978-1-922698-41-4 (pback)
ISBN 978-1-922473-43-1 (ebook)

Digital editions in association with ETT Imprint, Exile Bay

Copyright © 2022 Sandra J. Darroch

All rights reserved worldwide. No part of the book may be copied or changed in any format, sold, or used in any way other than what is outlined in this book, under any circumstances, without the prior written permission of the copyright-holder.

CONTENTS

INTRODUCTION

SYDNEY's NORTH SHORE was, and still is, a little world unto itself. Even now, it is distinctly different from the rest of Sydney, despite its attempts to move with the times.

Its origins have shaped it to this day: its first settlers were mainly of English or Scottish descent, coming from the better-off parts of Sydney's old Western Suburbs such as Strathfield, setting the tone for future arrivals, particularly after the North Shore railway line was constructed.

The North Shore is one of the top residential areas of Sydney. This book traces the development of the North Shore's behaviour and habits – particularly those which distinguish it from the Eastern Suburbs. It is not a "history book" – rather, it is an insider's personal view. One of my great-grandfathers, after retiring from his Pitt Street printing business moved to Turramurra when it was still "all bush" with no railway line. I myself grew up on the North Shore, went to school there, made long-lasting friendships and had a lot of fun. But I also observed it with a budding journalist's eye and experienced its faults - this is not a Politically Correct book.

In the old days, there were only two "top" Sydney enclaves: the North Shore and the Eastern Suburbs, apart from Hunters Hill. North Shore people in their leafy streets looked down on the Eastern Suburbs as being too ritzy, too racy, too affluent, too full of "reffos", and packed with flats rather than houses – in fact, the reincarnation of Sodom and Gomorrah.

Eastern Suburbs people. on the other hand, rarely crossed the Harbour Bridge over to the "boring, snooty" North Shore if they could help it. Things have changed a bit nowadays, but not that much.

The North Shore owed much of its existence to the arrival of the Railway in 1890, before which, would-be settlers, like my great-grandfather, had to get there via the West by horse and cart. But when the North Shore Railway Line was laid down, and later, in1932 the Harbour Bridge was opened, the North Shore came of age and became the blueprint for middle-class, conservative, affluent Australian suburbia.

But there was an important difference between The North Shore <u>Line</u> and <u>the</u> "North Shore." The North Shore Line started at Central Railway and ended up at Waitara, one stop north of Hornsby, but the "North Shore" started at Roseville and ended at Wahroonga, at Pierce's Corner, to be exact. Anything past Pierce's Corner was not "North Shore". At the southern extremity of the Lower North Shore, no suburbs before Roseville, such as Waverton, St Leonards or Chatswood were counted as "North Shore" either. The dividing line at the south was Boundary Street, marking very clearly the vast difference between Chatswood and Roseville. In between Roseville and Wahroonga were Lindfield, Killara, Gordon, Pymble, Turramurra, Warrawee, and Wahroonga: the "North Shore". Two relatively new suburbs, St Ives and East Lindfield, which were actually not on the "Line", squeaked in as "North Shore" too. But other suburbs, equally affluent and conservative, such as Mosman, were not "North Shore". They could be described as "North Side" but they were not "North Shore".

Certain North Shore suburbs have always ranked higher than others: Killara, and Wahroonga, on the Upper North Shore, have always been the top ones. But that wasn't all. In the early days, the Eastern side of the North Shore as the Line progressed north up to Pierce's Corner was the Right Side of the Tracks. Today, the Western side of the line is regarded as equally OK.

These days, the "North Shore" has blended in many peoples' minds into the "Northside" and thus encompasses many other suburbs situated around the northern side of the Harbour, and beyond. Nevertheless, to the true insider, the North Shore still starts at Roseville and ends at Wahroonga.

CHAPTER 1

PUT DOWN AT BIRTH

THE NORTH SHORE, when I arrived in April 1942, bang in the middle of World War Two, was in a state of suspended animation. This was because the Men had gone to fight the Japs, and what was left was a matriarchal society, waiting for the Men to return and the North Shore globe to turn again. This didn't mean that nothing happened or that nothing was done. Quite the contrary, the women on the North Shore were activated as never before. Not only did they have to run their households as usual, but they also had to repair the plumbing, mow the lawn, re-stock the coke heap ready to refill the coke heater, plus many other tasks previously looked after by the Man of the House. My mother fixed brown paper to the windows to prevent enemy planes catching sight of our kitchen light, and Mrs Martz next door filled her bathtub every day in case the water was cut off, but, as a two-year-old, I thought this was for all of us to get into the bath if the Japs arrived. Quite often the air-raid siren at the end of our street was turned on, to make sure it was still working, but no enemy planes ever flew over Roseville.

Nevertheless, with no new houses being built, many businesses lying idle, and no end of the War yet in sight, the North Shore was on hold.

Dozing beneath a mosquito net in my bassinet next to the other babies, tended by our mothers in the garden of the Tonga maternity cottage hospital in Addison Road, Roseville, I was blissfully unaware that the Japs had invaded Darwin two months previously, on February 29 when 242 Jap planes had hit the city. (Many North Shore people always called them the "Japs" during the War, and even after the War ended – until they began making cheap household gadgets that actually worked. Then the North Shore started calling them "the Japanese").

Nevertheless, everyone in Roseville was scared the Japs would invade. As I moved on from breast and bottle feeding to more solid foods. I remained unaware that between February 1942 and November 1943, during the Pacific war, the Australian mainland, domestic airspace, offshore islands, and coastal shipping were attacked at least 111 times by enemy Navy, Airforce and Army aircraft.

The closest the enemy got to the North Shore was in late May 1942 when three midget submarines from the Japanese fleet entered Sydney Harbour. Fortunately for us, they were intercepted, and one was sunk, while the other two were later salvaged and tied up at a wharf after the War ended, and I, aged three, and my grandmother, along with many other sightseers, climbed down into one of them to inspect it. It was really claustrophobic.

After the attack on Sydney Harbour, my mother's gynaecologist, Dr Kate Cunningham, a baritone-voiced woman, urged my mother to escape with her up the Blue Mountains to avoid the Japs. But my mother chose to remain in the garden suburb of Roseville, running her household, looking after a new baby, doing all the other chores her doctor husband, away in New Guinea used to do when he was home, not to mention walking to the shops with her Ration Book instead of driving: to save her precious petrol coupons.

The wives also did their bit for the War, knitting warming balaclavas and woollen socks and scarves for the Men away in the Tropics. What the brave Men, sweating in the tropical heat, did with these knitted tributes is not known. My mother, as the wife of a young doctor away at the War, was inducted into the local Ladies' Auxiliary and spent many sunny afternoons knitting for the troops on the front verandah with the other Auxiliary members who indoctrinated her into the ways of the North Shore, which, as a newcomer to the area, she gratefully absorbed.

She learned that North Shore girls should not go to the public (State) school and instead have their names put down (at birth, if possible) for the top preparatory school, Cromehurst, at Lindfield, and for Abbotsleigh at Wahroonga, the best Anglican girls' school in Sydney. Presbyterian Ladies' College, PLC, at Pymble, was alright if a family happened to be Presbyterian, and there was also Ravenswood, at Gordon – for Methodists and other (non-Catholic) religions. For boys, the No.1 Anglican school was Shore, despite being located at North Sydney, outside the "North Shore", which was, and still is, a GPS (Great Public School), but at a pinch there was Barker College, at Hornsby (now co-ed) also Anglican but not GPS, and Knox Grammar, also not GPS, for Presbyterians. There were no Catholic mothers in the Ladies' Auxiliary, and indeed, there were few Catholic schools on the North Shore at that time.

Occasionally some of the Men would return on Leave briefly – my very existence, and that of my sister Steph were testament to this.

But it wasn't until the War ended and the Men finally came Home that our North Shore world came into its full flowering.

CHAPTER 2

THE MEN COME HOME

WHEN THE MEN came Home to the North Shore, the sound of male voices and the smell **of** backyard gum leaves burning-off at weekends permeated the air. A fervour of home renovations and gardening erupted as North Shore Ration Books were gradually put away and affluence started to open wallets and handbags. The North Shore led the way.

Almost as soon as my father came through the front gate back from New Guinea, he started planning renovations to our classic purple-brick Californian bungalow. The brown Feltex in the hall and living room was ripped up and replaced with pastel green carpet. The wooden beams in the ceilings were pulled out and a new, modern, ready-made plaster ceiling installed. The leadlight windows were reglazed with plain glass, and a gas fire was put in the fireplace instead of the old coke fire. Later, my father cement-rendered the purple brick and painted the walls cream. A classic Californian bungalow it now no longer resembled. The "coal hole" down the back next to the outdoor toilet was scrapped and replaced by an aviary for budgerigars, and an indoor toilet was installed in the upstairs bathroom.

Renovating meant Saturday morning visits to the major North Shore hardware store, Benjamins, at Chatswood. Because I was now old enough to walk, my father defied convention and took me, a girl, with him. On entering that masculine bailiwick, I discovered a new and exciting world that was a stark contrast to the all-female environment I had previously known. Benjamins had a culture of matey camaraderie, where the rat-a-tat--tat of nails being poured into the weighing scales, the sawing of planks of wood, and the smells of fresh rope and turpentine mingled with conversation about hammers and spanners and sand-and-cement. The hardware store was also the local watering hole, where the men confirmed golf dates for later in the day. It provided the camaraderie the returned soldiers craved after the War.

On our regular trips to the hardware store I was witness to how Australia's way-of-life began to change. Paint was improving, with new acrylics replacing oils which had never really dried, and a whole swatch of brighter pastel colours to choose from. Sand and cement began to be packed and sold in ready-mixed bags. Nails and screws started to be displayed in pre-packed cellophane instead of in bulk brown paper bags, and power drills and saws began to appear. Electric radiators and gas fires banished the old coke-stove – and the coke heap itself. Spanking-new barbecues came on the market, and Hills Hoists later replaced the old rope or wire clotheslines – and the clothesprop man.

But along with this burst of post-war modernisation, we also suffered regular power blackouts, usually just when my mother was cooking the chops on the Early Kooka gas stove with its kookaburra logo. "That dratted Mr Conde," my mother would exclaim, cursing the head of the electricity company as she once again lit the kerosene lantern and put a match to the little methylated spirit stove. (Actually, Mr Conde eventually did a lot to get Sydney's power system working efficiently. The man my mother should have been cursing was Mr McGirr the Labor Premier).

Nevertheless, progress marched on, and over time, as the 40's turned into the 50's, women started patronising the hardware store, too. The male shop assistants treated them in the same relaxed, egalitarian manner they did their male customers, and the matey atmosphere of the hardware store lived on. If a female customer wanted to put up a cupboard in her kitchen, but wasn't quite sure what type of bracket to buy, or what door-handles to choose, she was given friendly advice by the man behind the counter, who went out of his way to pull out as many different examples as he could. And if she wasn't exactly sure of what to call the "thingummy" that fitted on the end of a towel-rail, the other, male, customers chimed in with their advice.

The backyard shed-cum-workshop was an outreach of that hardware store blokey culture. Mates dropped in to my father's garage-workshop with a bottle of beer for a yarn at the weekend or on their way home from work on the double-decker. Further departing from convention, my father allowed me down to his workshop after school, where he showed me how to saw wood properly, how to choose the right nail, and how to screw hinges on. Sitting amongst the wood shavings on the workshop floor behind the circular saw, I listened to the blokes' conversation. They rarely, if ever, mentioned the War, nor did they talk much about their work. There was no discussion about personal matters, unlike my mother's, grandmother's and aunts' conversations up in the kitchen. The blokes down in the workshop talked about their cars, sometimes about sport, but more often about the North Shore preoccupation with home and property topics. They never talked about sex and rarely mentioned politics – apart from when Mr Chifley threatened to nationalise the banking system, and then that Nice Mr Menzies hove into view. However, I do recall one late afternoon when a friend of my father's hopped off the bus and sat down on a wooden crate in the workshop over a beer with my father and tried to get him to join what came to be known as the New Guard. "Some of us are getting worried the Commies are infiltrating our government" I heard his friend say. But my father said he wasn't interested in the New Guard – he still belonged to the University Regiment, which was actually part of the <u>Old</u> Guard.

My mother became progressively concerned that I was spending too much time in my father's shed, and she tried to lure me back to the house to learn knitting and other domestic vocations "like other little girls". So I did knitting too, which I quite enjoyed.

Going to the hardware store on Saturdays with my father opened my eyes to the first shoots of burgeoning post-war affluence, but while Benjamins at Chatswood embraced the modern, post-war methods of cellophane packaging and other new-fangled marketing practices, the smaller local shops were

8

slower to catch up. Indeed, the Roseville shops on the non-Pacific Highway side of the railway line remained for some years more-or-less the same as they had been before the war began.

Our weekday trips to the Roseville shops usually started at the Post Office, then the butcher's shop next door where I played in the sawdust on the floor, then came Warrens, the fruiterers. Next was Moran & Cato, the grocers, where shoppers would stand at the counter and order a pound of sugar, or a pound of bran, and the assistant would measure it out and weigh it and put it into brown paper bags. The Isobel was next door, a haberdashery shop with dark polished wooden counters and one of those vacuum systems for sending cash to the back of the shop and spurting back receipts. Rows of Silko embroidery thread made a rainbow display, and every kind of safety pin, knitting needle and wool was available. The two sisters who ran the Isobel provided a corsetry service, and I liked to examine the display torsos encased in their pink corsets with whalebones slipped into little slotted ribs sewn into the sides.

After the Isobel was Mr Dunne, the chemist, a plump, smiling gentleman with a bald, shiny head and a pink face. My mother would sidle up to the counter and try to get one of the girls to serve her when she whispered "Modess" (sanitary napkins) to them. The ham-and-beef shop with its noisy ham-slicing machine was next, then the newsagent, selling *The Sydney Morning Herald*, *The Telegraph* and, in the afternoon, the *Sun* and the *Mirror*. Most North Shire people who prided themselves as being safely middle-class, preferred the *Sydney Morning Herald* over the *Tele* which was regarded as a bit Lower Class, and some people, getting off the train in the evening would buy the *Sun*, but rarely the *Mirror*. Magazines started to proliferate on the newsagent's shelves and on the posters outside the shop. Some, like the *Australian Women's Weekly*, had been on sale before the War, but others, such as car and sports publications, grew steadily in the post-war affluence. Next to the newsagent, on the corner of the main shopping block, was the milkbar where vanilla milkshakes or malted milk were served in metal containers. Ice-cream came in cones or in cardboard buckets, eaten with little wooden spoons. The suburban shops were a little slow in embracing the post-war boom, but eventually even they began to modernise. Gradually, more and more goods arrived pre-packed, and the ritual of the weighing machine declined.

The post-war affluence seeping across Australia had arrived on the North Shore a little earlier than most other areas of Sydney, apart from the Eastern Suburbs and enclaves like Hunters Hill which had always been affluent, although over in the Eastern Suburbs, dotted among the mansions were lots of rent-controlled blocks of flats occupied by refugees from the War in Europe. The Eastern Suburbs also had a lot of privately-owned flats, whereas the North Shore prided itself on its quarter-acre blocks and many larger gardens. In those days, everybody knew everybody in our street, and front doors stayed open all day. Neighbours popped in and out and the children rode their tricycles and bikes on the footpath and played together in each other's gardens.

The North Shore had avidly embraced the Post-War Boom. Indeed, it was in the Boom avant garde. It led the way to the 1950s and 60s suburban prosperity which gradually seeped into the rest of Australia. As well as cars in the garage, power drills and motor mowers in the shed, washing machines and even washing-up machines (as dishwashers were then called), began to make their way into the modern cream-and-green North Shore kitchen, alongside the Silent Knight refrigerator. Then came the radiogram in the living-room, and at long last, the TV.

CHAPTER 3

AMO BILLYO

EDUCATION was a priority for North Shore residents. Private schools, in the early Post-war period, were the natural source of education for North Shore children, although "Education" in the sense of learning about maths, science, art, literature, geography or any other of the disciplines was not, at that time the main priority. The emphasis in the private school sector was on "Meeting and mixing with the right people." If a parent wanted his or her child to be "educated", there was a handful of excellent High Schools on the North Shore: Hornsby Girls High, and down at North Sydney there were North Sydney Boys and North Sydney Girls High. That many of the graduates of these high schools soared to the top at university later on didn't ruffle the feathers of the parents of private school pupils in those days -- they prized the excellent sporting facilities and spacious grounds of their chosen Private School.

School started for me with kindergarten in the Roseville Scouts Hall where we four-year-olds sat on the floor in front of an enormous Union Jack displayed behind the platform on which the teacher stood. My only memory of my first, and only, day at the Scouts Hall is that of the boy pupils preventing the girls from going to the toilet. I wet my pants going home on the bus and told my Mother I was never going back to the Scouts Hall.

Next, my Mother, following the edicts of the Women's Auxiliary, which still met to knit socks and scarves, now for the aborigines in the Far West Homes, enrolled me at Cromehurst, the preparatory school for Abbotsleigh, for which I had been put down almost at birth.

Recalling the traumas of not being able to visit the toilet at the Scouts Hall, I reluctantly allowed my mother to dress me in the requisite winter uniform ready for my first day at

Cromehurst. The winter uniform consisted of a heavy brown serge tunic, long brown woollen socks, brown lace-up shoes, and a brown velour velvet hat with a crest on the hatband which said something like "Amo Billyo Coggitate", which, I was told, was Latin for "Think on Things That Are Lovely". Suitably garbed, I then panicked and crept away and climbed into the hull of the sailing boat my parents kept under the house. In the darkness of its hull, I was invisible in my dark brown uniform and remained hidden in the boat all day, impervious to my mother's frantic calls as she hunted high and low. Finally, hunger drove me out, and after a scolding, I was persuaded to attend Cromehurst next day.

Cromehurst was in Lindfield, and to get there I had to walk down to our street corner , cross Archbold Road (which bore hardly any traffic because most people had yet to have cars) and catch the bus that toiled hour-in-hour-out between Roseville station and Lindfield stations, driven by Bill the Bus Driver. (In those days it was deemed perfectly safe for a four- or five-year-old to take the bus by him or herself, unaccompanied).

Bill was a fleshy man with black hairs that grew out of his ears and his nostrils, and he never waited for us if we were late and running frantically along the footpath towards the bus. He did, however, break his rule to wait for the Catholic kids who lived in the ramshackle house up the hill with the paspalum-infested front yard and the broken fence. Bill, you see, was a Catholic, and he made sure the Catholic kids got the best seats. Arriving at Lindfield station we got out, and, minus the Catholic kids who went off to a kindergarten on the other side of the Line, we walked in a crocodile down to the Cromehurst kindergarten in the church hall across the street from the Big School.

The kindergarten was run by Miss Hogg, a kindly woman who called us "little people" instead of "children", which I liked. There, we learned the alphabet, phonetically, with a big chart that said "A says "a" for apple"… "X says "xxxx" for "the end of box"", down to "Z says "zzz" for zebra" until we were sufficiently proficient with the alphabet to go across to the main school to recite our ABC to the Headmistress, Mrs Hume-Smith.

If we got it right, Mrs Hume-Smith gave us a jellybean. Instead of reciting "S says "sss" for snake" I said "S says "sss" for Sandra" and Mrs Hume-Smith rewarded me with two jellybeans.

Finally, next summer, we went up to Transition in the Big School. Our summer uniforms at kindergarten had been a pale-yellow cotton smock with embroidered yolks, and brown linen hats with wide brims, tied under the chin in a bow. By Transition, the smock was replaced with a proper tunic with a belt.

The Cromehurst Big School was in a bungalow with wide verandas, set in a garden surrounded by hedges, and planted with tall pine and palm trees. At the front was a rose garden where Mrs Hume-Smith's husband, who had retired from the Indian civil service, tended his roses. On the veranda was an enormous elephant's foot from India, which was used as an umbrella stand.

Transition was run by Miss Boden, a kinder teacher it would be hard to find. We did marble painting out in the courtyard under the palm trees and lots of drawing. I was in my element. One day, a fellow pupil, Robin, showed me the right way to draw houses with window curtains. (Robin was, years later, to commit suicide after suffering postnatal depression.)

The next year, we were moved into 1B. On the first day we were given a little story book to learn how to read. "Dot has a hoop", the story began. I worked out the first words phonetically, wondering why Dot would want to have a hoop, seeing that the only hoops I knew about were those things that fitted into the tops of mosquito nets. Then I got the hang of reading, and by the next page I was racing through the story of what Dot did with her hoop. I was immediately put up to 1A and became the youngest pupil in that class of strangers, girls, none of whom I knew. But I still had my friend Jennifer from my previous year, and we sat together at lunchtime and cracked open our hard-boiled eggs on each other's heads.

At playtime we trooped into the school kitchen with our mugs taken out of our leather satchels ready for a cup of milk, and then we'd go out to swing ourselves over the parallel bars.

Sometimes gangs of girls played war games in the hedges around the school, sticking leaves from the hedges on their foreheads to make themselves look ferocious. One day there was a sensation at playtime when a girl vomited purple all over the path that wound round the schoolhouse; she had been treated with gentian violet for worms.

One morning we were told in Assembly that Mrs Hume-Smith, had fallen very ill, and we were all asked to bring flowers to make her better. So at sunrise next morning Mimi (my grandmother) and I went down to the bottom of our garden where the nasturtiums rampaged over the rubbish heap. I could hardly choose between the orange nasturtiums and the yellow ones and I picked hundreds of them, and also their leaves, where little beads of dew rolled around on them like tiny balls of mercury. My grandmother gathered up the flowers in her apron and we found some tissue paper in the kitchen drawer and wrapped the flowers up. Then I raced off to the bus, eager to help Mrs Hume-Smith get better.

When I reached the school kitchen, where all the flowers from the other pupils were piled up on the table, I saw many very grand bouquets, and boxes of orchids, wrapped in cellophane and tied with ribbon. Later, I crept along the hallway that led to Mrs Hume-Smith's bedroom to see if my flowers were making her better. I could see Mrs Hume-Smith in her bed propped up by pillows, talking to her housekeeper about the flowers.

"How kind of Sir John and Lady …. to send these roses," she was saying, opening one of the cellophane-covered boxes.

"What are these funny little flowers, Mrs Walker?" Mrs Hume-Smith then asked the housekeeper, pointing to my bunch of nasturtiums. "Would you like them for your sitting-room?" I crept back down the hallway.

Some girls came down from the Upper North Shore to attend Cromehurst, and one of them, the daughter of a well-known Judge, befriended me. One afternoon she told me that my Nanny had said I was to come home to her place to play. I didn't have a "Nanny", so I assumed she meant my grandmother, and I

14

hopped happily into the back of a big shiny black car that was waiting outside the school and we set off to her home in Killara. The car was driven by a man wearing a uniform and a cap, who didn't speak to us. When we reached my schoolfriend's enormous house, the front door was opened by the housekeeper. Nobody else was home. We went down the darkened hallway to a vast kitchen equipped with marble-topped tables and grey cupboards, and were given glasses of orange juice and told to go outside into the garden and play. By the time it was about 5pm and shadows were creeping across the manicured lawn towards the pencil pines, I began to feel scared and started to cry. The housekeeper noticed my tears and asked me if my mother was coming to pick me up. When I shook my head she asked me to tell her where I lived and she checked the phonebook and rang my mother who had at first thought I'd been kept in for doing something naughty, but she was now so concerned she was about to ring the police. She hadn't dreamed I'd been kidnapped by my classmate who was obviously an extremely lonely little girl.

Going to the Easter Show was one of the big events in our lives and everybody talked about it at school. Mrs Hume-Smith, now recovered, as a result of the mountain of flowers she had received, holding assembly each morning, would always ask if anyone had some news to tell the school, So after our visit to the Easter Show my sister Steph put up her hand: "Yes Mrs Hume-Smith," she began. "My sister got lost at the Easter Show." I squirmed with embarrassment. I had indeed got lost at the Show. To this day I can remember the big hand of the policeman holding on to mine as we wove our way through the crowd to the Lost Children's Tent where I, and a straggle of other, tearful, Lost Children, were coaxed into eating ice-creams and drinking lemonade while we waited for our parents to reclaim us.

By the time I was six I was in Prep, taught by Mrs Hume-Smith herself, who was very strict and wielded the Magic Ruler, which hurt our hands. The final year at Cromehurst was called Prep because it was in preparation for us going on to Abbotsleigh, or, in the case of the few Presbyterian pupils, PLC. In Prep, being the youngest in the class, I was often very much at sea with my lessons, especially arithmetic. We moved on to pounds, shillings and pence and I simply couldn't get the hang of it. I went home that night and told my father, who sat me on his knee and went through pounds, shillings, and pence until I knew how to do it.

On the other hand, however, I was good at English. One day we were told to write a little essay about paint for a competition BALM Paint was holding for all children in NSW. My long experience of the hardware store put me in good stead and my essay won First Prize.

As well as reading, writing and arithmetic, we had Speech Training with Mrs Parkinson who had red lips like two poinsettia leaves and taught us how to say "How now, brown cow" over and over again, which of course we already knew how to pronounce, along with a lot of other things we North Shore kids knew from home, such as you never said "Pleased to meet you" instead of "How do you do?" Nor did you say "marone" instead of "maroon" or "serviette" instead of "table napkin" or "Pardon?" instead of "Excuse me?" Nor should you ever park your car on your front lawn.

Despite the Magic Ruler, Mrs Hume Smith ran a very pleasant and successful operation. We pupils were happy and thought school was fun, and Mrs Hume-Smith handled the social rankings of her students' parents with aplomb. When I was in Prep, my mother had another baby, Ingrid. When, several months after Ingrid's birth I summoned the courage to go up to the kitchen window at playtime and tell Mrs Hume-Smith this news, she admonished me: "You should have told me the moment she was born," she scolded. "She should have been put down at birth for Cromehurst, but now I'll have her put down immediately."

CHAPTER 4

THE BIRTHDAY PARTY

THE SATURDAY AFTERNOON BIRTHDAY PARTY was an intrinsic element of North Shore lore. After I started school the main thing I did most Saturdays, apart from visiting the hardware store with my father, was to accompany my mother to a gift shop to buy a birthday present for that Saturday afternoon's Party Girl. If you liked the Party Girl you bought her a china pony or bunny for her dressing table. If she wasn't very nice, you bought her a handkerchief. Then you went home, wrapped your present in pastel tissue paper and tied it with a satin ribbon, with a birthday card, had lunch and put on your party dress. Until you were about 11, your dress had to be made by your mother - dresses bought from David Jones or Farmers for younger girls were frowned-on by the grandmothers who stood at the door when you arrived to ring the door chimes at the Party Girl's house in your party dress, your angora wool bolero, white ankle socks and black patent leather shoes. "Did Mummy make your dress?" the grandmothers would enquire, nodding approval if the answer was in the affirmative.

Many North Shore houses we visited for parties were two-storeyed and we would rush upstairs to the Party Girl's bedroom to watch her unwrap the presents and display them on her frilly bedspread. Sometimes, if we looked out her bedroom window, we could see, glaring glumly through a back window, the Party Girl's Brother, banished from the afternoon's proceedings.

Then we'd tumble downstairs and out into the back garden where the lawn was invariably manicured couch grass, dotted with crazy paving pathways.

First, we played games in the garden organised by the Party Girl's father who had nobly foregone his Saturday afternoon golf game. Treasure hunts were popular. We also played putting the tail on the donkey and skipping games if there was a paved area. One party was memorable after I dropped my bracelet into the Party Girl's fishpond and her father took the opportunity to drain and clean out the pond. We all jumped in, and, to our mothers' dismay, got mud all over our party dresses. If it happened to be raining on the day of a Party, we played indoor games such as Pass the Parcel, and Things on the Tray. This was a game where a tea tray containing a melange of items like buttons and a flower, a cup, a ball etc was passed around. Then the tray was taken away and we had to write down how many of the objects we could remember were on the tray. Birthday Parties in those days were simple affairs.

Following the games came the Afternoon Tea. On sunny days, everyone flocked back inside to the dining room where frankfurter sausages and hundreds-and-thousands sandwiches awaited us on the table under the balloons hanging from the wrought-iron lamp or the chandelier. After the food came the films which were projected by the Party Girl's father onto a portable screen hired for the occasion. Charlie Chaplin was the favourite, although we occasionally saw a Buster Keaton film, which I preferred because I got tired of all the party guests screaming how they loved Charlie Chaplin. We sat watching these films in mahogany and brocade armchairs usually from Beard Watsons. There was often an oval gold-framed mirror on the wall, and floral-patterned carpet. The kitchens were all equipped with modern electric or gas stoves, usually in the fashionable green-and-cream kitchen colour scheme, and sometime there was even a dishwasher.

Some girls' mothers went out a lot to lunch parties and were photographed for the *Telegraph* or the *Sydney Morning Herald's* women's sections' social pages, lunching at Princes. One Party Girl's mother used to catch the train at Roseville every week, dressed in a smart suit with a hat and a little veil. She was off to the Randwick races. She didn't have a housekeeper and I noticed at her daughter's Party that the furniture had dust on it.

At 5pm it was time for the fathers who had finished playing golf to come and pick up their daughters from that afternoon's Party, and we left, clutching a balloon and a piece of the birthday cake wrapped in a paper napkin. On Sunday morning we had to sit down and write a Thank You note to the Party Girl's mother. We had lessons at school on the right way to write such a letter. The first rules were "You must never start your letter with the personal pronoun 'I'" and "You Must Never Mention the Food". You should, on the other hand, praise something about the party, such as the beautiful flowers or the wonderful games. We were taught to sign our letter "Yours sincerely" and to only use "Yours faithfully" when writing to an official whom one didn't know.

The adults on the North Shore partied too, of course. My parents held an annual Christmas cocktail party where my father, being by now a consultant anaesthetist, invited his fellow anaesthetists and the surgeons he gave anaesthetics for, to come for finger food and cocktails at Christmas time. Many of these guests lived in the Eastern Suburbs, and for these medicos, "crossing the Bridge" was equivalent to slumming it. But they approached my parents' cocktail parties in an indulgent spirit and they and their wives were soon kicking up their heels, downing g-and-t's and flirting with each other's partners.

When I was about 11, I became a junior cocktail waitress, carrying a plate of savouries around, threading my way through the legs of the guests and adroitly avoiding the pinches aimed at my bottom by certain august surgeons.

CHAPTER 5

TIME FLIES FASTER THAN
THE WEAVER'S SHUTTLE

IT WAS TIME to go to Abbotsleigh. I was seven, going on eight. and although my name had not been put down at birth, but at the age of two, I was readily inducted into this Anglican enclave sited on the Pacific Highway at Wahroonga.

The exclusive private girls' schools on Sydney's North Shore in those days were still principally established to produce well-behaved young ladies. I was strictly reminded of this when, a few years later, I, and a handful of fellow students were to be awarded prizes at the annual Speech Day. We were called into the headmistress's study and told: "Girls, you may well have won prizes for your academic achievement, but the principal aim of Abbotsleigh is to produce good wives and mothers."

Prior to my first day at Abbotsleigh was the task of getting outfitted for my school uniform, a task which was to become a bi-annual ritual event as the summer or winter school holidays came to an end. Farmers department store was our mother's choice for school uniforms - David Jones was regarded as a bit too Eastern Suburbs for my mother's more sober North Shore tastes. To get to Farmers, we had to catch the bus or train into Wynyard and then walk along George Street and up Market Street.

For these shopping expeditions, my sister and I would dress up in our best frocks, and our mother would wear a suit, hat and gloves. We would arrive at Farmers around 11am and go directly up to the Uniforms Department to be fitted out with our new Abbotsleigh summer or winter uniforms and gym tunics. Green was the colour for both summer and winter Abbotsleigh uniforms in those days, light green for summer, dark green for winter: a colour not particularly suited to those girls with sallow complexions. Our gym slips were pale yellow and had silk tassels representing the colour of the House a girl belonged to: maroon for Macquarie House, Yellow for Sturt, and purple for Wentworth.

Our new panama straw (for summer) and velour (for winter) hats had green-and-gold hatbands embossed in Latin saying "Tempus celerius radio fugit", which, we were told, meant "Time Flies Faster than the Weaver's Shuttle". This adage still puzzles me. Logically and mathematically, it is untenable, or is it a maxim that implies that you'd better hurry up and find a husband, or you'll end up an old maid?

After our uniform fittings, it was up to the store's dining-room where we had lunch - starched white tablecloths, a waitress to take our order (roast lamb followed by ice-cream with caramel topping, served in metal bowls with little handles).

Then came the new shoes. Farmers' Shoe Department was ruled by a seven-foot-tall, very thin martinet of a woman in ultra-high-heels and silver-bleached hair done in a tight chignon. Our feet were measured on those metal sliding frames which are a rarity nowadays, and the shop assistants would bring out boxes of shoes, one pair at a time, until our school shoes and sandshoes for gym and sport were chosen.

My mother would then go in search of shoes for herself, while we'd rush off to the X-ray machines to take multiple views of our skeletal feet, glowing green. What those X-rays were doing to us - and future generations - was far from our minds.

Next was the Fabrics Department where our mother would, like all the other female shoppers, go into a semi-trance, her eyes vaguely scanning the bales of material, while she pensively fingered the velvets and cottons. Time dragged on and we were finally taken into the ladies' powder-room where a matronly woman in a white tunic stood by a table laid out with fresh towels.

As evening began to fall, came the walk back along George Street to Wynyard. As we approached the crossing opposite Wynyard station, an unforgettable aroma of boronia wafted towards us. A group of gypsies seated on the pavement with baskets full of wild-flowers and violets would push sprigs of fragrant brown boronia under our noses. It never occurred to us how gypsies had got all the way from Eastern Europe to Sydney (though they were probably just Irish immigrants from the Paddington slums). My mother usually gave them sixpence.

Each new term, we had to get our new train ticket, and this meant religion began to rear its head: if you went to a North Shore school which was of the same religious persuasion as you, such as Abbotsleigh being Church of England, and if you were Church of England, then you would receive from the department of transport a green cardboard train ticket to put in a little leather ticket holder attached to the handle of your Globite suitcase. This indicated you travelled free. But if you happened to be Presbyterian or Methodist (there was never a Catholic at Abbotsleigh as far as I know) and were nevertheless going to Abbotsleigh, you had to have a little metal "ticket" which you had to pay for and attach to a bracelet on your wrist. The same arrangement went for other schools: for example, if you went to Presbyterian Ladies College (PLC) and were Presbyterian, you got a free green cardboard ticket, but if you were Church of England, or one of the other faiths, you had to have a metal ticket.

Suitably equipped for school, we travelled by train each day up the North Shore Line, only a few Abbotsleigh girls getting on the train before Roseville, the official start of the proper North Shore. One or two girls, came from Chatswood, and a few girls got the train coming the other way down from Thornleigh, which was not counted as "North Shore".

Gone were our old leather satchels, replaced with gleaming brown Globite suitcases. We soon got the knack of standing with our legs straddling our Globites, talking together in nonchalant groups at the far end of the station past the secretaries and businessmen who were waiting for the down train into town. I usually caught the train from Roseville, but sometimes, if I'd missed the bus to Roseville I took it on its way back to Lindfield station.

Quite often while we waited for our train we would see a Big Sister of one of our schoolfriends. I was told by one of my friends who had a Big Sister that when a Big Sister left school something very important happened to her, but she didn't say what, and I imagined the Big Sister undergoing some kind of medical procedure to do with being old enough to have babies. It turned out, however, that what my friend was referring to was: Going to Miss Hales. This was where the Big Sisters were inducted into the process of becoming a Secretary, spending a whole year learning typing and shorthand at Miss Hales' business college in town.

The Big Sisters wore grey or tartan pleated skirts in winter with twinsets with frilly lace or Peter Pan collars. In summer they wore cotton skirts with lots of petticoats, sometimes even hoops.

There were plenty of private school boys from Knox and Barker on the up-train and we saw the Grammar and Shore boys on the other side of the station waiting to catch the down-train to North Sydney or on to Town Hall where they would alight to reach their schools. The Barker boys, riding up the Line with us towards Hornsby, were the brashest, tilting their boaters on the back of their heads and flirting with the older girls from the Senior School. But at the age of eight I wasn't the slightest bit interested in boys, indeed the only boy I knew, our Sunday school attendee neighbour, had recently deserted me and Steph to join the all boys' gang, riding their bikes, shouting rude things at us girls and bellowing "Woollah, woollah, bang bang bang. We belong to the Roseville gang."

The outside world didn't impinge on us much - the Korean war began in 1950, and so did the Snowy Mountains Hydro-Electric Scheme, and though we heard our parents talk about them, we didn't take much notice. No, the things we were more interested in at that stage was collecting scraps depicting baskets of flowers and pasting them on to our newly brown-paper-covered exercise books, and packing our Globites with a zip-up pencil case, a set of Derwent colour pencils and a Parker fountain pen, and we also had to have a Slazenger Blue Bird tennis racquet.

On my first day at Abbotsleigh I had been told that I was too young to go into third form and that I had to repeat second form. This meant I would be back with my earliest Cromehurst friends, and I was glad to return to them, though my former best friend, Jennifer, went on to Ravenswood. In those days, the Junior School, with its surprisingly progressive headmistress, Mrs Palmer, was still sited in the Senior School grounds, housed in an old building with verandas on two levels. Across from the Junior School was the big modern red brick building that housed the Senior School, set in immaculate lawns, leading down to the Upper and Lower ovals, a seemingly endless array of tennis courts, and the Glen, a gully filled with old gum trees, winding paths and bamboo plantations.

Boarders, girls coming from wealthy grazier families to have their manners ironed out, were a new phenomenon to me. Some of them were very rough on arrival, asking "Miss, can I go to the dumpty?" instead of asking "Please may I be excused?" Despite living cooped up at school, with, in those days only two "free" weekends per term, the boarders were a cheerful bunch. They spent a lot of time sucking condensed milk out of tubes because they said the school food was awful, and they told us about farm life. One boarder regaled us with "Jack and Mary in the Dairy…" and later went on to write romantic fiction for Mills & Boone.

The Junior School, run by Mrs Palmer, provided an excellent basic education. By the end of Fifth Form, we, or most of us, could read and write fluently, spell and parse accurately, write short compositions and recite some poetry. We could draw a map of Australia, using a plastic shape which had wiggly rivers cut into it. The kings and queens of England were familiar names. We city girls also learned a lot about country Australia from Mrs Palmer who had apparently been born somewhere in the country. She had given us a broad view of Australian history - the graziers, squatters, explorers and so on. We also did projects on wool and wheat, which in those days were Australia's main exports. The Wool Board happily supplied all the schools with little samples of combed wool which we stuck into our project books. We were taught to write as legibly as possible, using Copy Books which forced us to write with the approved slope to each letter. I felt this was not a sensible way to help children to write legibly because when they grew up they would all find their own style. So I put up my hand and said so to Mrs Palmer, and, to her credit, she then did away with the copy books. We were also taught about native plants and animals, wore sprigs of wattle on our lapels on August 1, the date in those days of Wattle Day, and felt proud that we were Australians - in a completely unpretentious and unselfconscious way. Above all, some of us, at least, learned to think for ourselves.

One thing Mrs Palmer did that was particularly unusual was that she held regular courts of law in the classroom, rearranging the desks into a semi-circle and appointing a judge and jury to hear any case of alleged bullying by the class (or, as we said at Abbotsleigh, "form") bullies who were good at tennis and bossed us about. Those bullies were little savages but no doubt turned out to be nice North Shore matrons in the end, running the school tuckshop, or holding fund-raising afternoon teas. Today, perhaps they would be using Social Media.

Sometimes, however, we took the law into our own hands. The bullies had been harassing me a lot, stuffing leaves down my neck on the Lower Oval, and scraping my legs against the stone coping of the driveway at the front gate of the school as we waited in a crocodile to cross the Pacific Highway on our way back to Wahroonga station in the afternoons. My father, spotting my grazed legs, asked me how that had happened. I explained and he said "Those girls need a good kick in the shins." Next morning I put on my heavy winter shoes and when I arrived at school I told one of the bullies that I had a secret to tell them at Recess. They were to queue up behind the sewing hut and I would reveal the secret to them one-by-one.

At Recess I told each of them to line up and then one-by-one to come around the corner of the sewing hut where I would reveal the secret. On arrival at the point of revelation, I took each gang member by the shoulders and kicked her very hard in the shins with my heavy winter shoes. "Now you won't ever bully me again," I told each of them. "Go away to the end of the hut and do not tell the others."

That evening I told my father: "I did it!"

"What did you do?" he asked.

"I gave them all a good kick in the shins, like you said" I replied.

"I didn't mean you should do that literally," he replied. "It was just a figure of speech."

The only weakness in our primary school education was when we went into fourth form and were taught by Miss G., who sank below Mrs Palmer's high Plimsoll Line because her grey petticoats drooped at least ten inches below the hem of her dress, and she dunked her morning tea biscuit in her tea and only knew two things to teach us. One was the names of the railway stations between Central and Wallerawang, which she made us chant daily. The only other thing she taught us was a song called "Lights are Gleaming on the Grand Canal. Come, come, come and see the carniv-al", which she made us sing every day, much to the annoyance of Mrs Palmer, whose classroom was next door, and who could hear her precious former pupils degenerating into mindless idiots. Fortunately, we had our final year in the Junior School, Fifth Form, once again with Mrs Palmer.

Such was our formal education. What we had really been learning was how to be a member of our North Shore, middle-to-upper- middle class tribe. It was drummed into us in assembly each morning that to be an Abbotsleigh girl was to be privileged. "But with privilege comes responsibility".

CHAPTER 6

THE NORTH SHORE GARDEN

THE NORTH SHORE, even today, despite the gradual demise of the family tennis court, and the influx of some high-rise, especially along the Highway and the Line, is renowned for its gardens. Indeed, it has well-earned the sobriquet the "Leafy North Shore". The further up the Line you travel, the more spacious and manicured are the gardens, although there were, and still are, many smaller, quarter-acre blocks with well-tended gardens all the way up to Hornsby.

Strict protocols have always applied to North Shore gardens. Most were, and still are, grassed with couch, the politically correct grass for the North Shore, even though it breeds prickly bindyeyes in profusion. Buffalo grass has always been infradig, and paspalum deemed completely beyond the North Shore paling fence. Mowing all this grass entailed, in the early days, the use of a hardy push mower, but gradually motor mowers, driven by petrol and hard weekend labour, usually by the Man of the House, came into vogue, along with the Mower Man who tended the larger gardens farther up the North Shore line.

North Shore plants, particularly in the old days, leaned toward the English varieties: roses, chrysanthemums, poppies, magnolias, stocks, pansies, May bushes, willows... The manicured couch lawn was habitually interspersed with rose garden beds and paving stone pathways, and was mowed religiously. Virtually the only Australian native vegetation was the ubiquitous eucalypt, although some North Shore gardens today pride themselves on being "All Native".

Although our Roseville garden was by no means palatial, being just the front and back regions of a typical suburban quarter-acre block, it nevertheless shaped our lives and inspired our imaginations, it fostered countless intricate games and was a vital part of our young universe.

Our front garden had a wisteria-covered front fence, two "Christmas bush" trees with their red miniature star-like flowers, and the hydrangeas along the edge of the veranda. Under the May bush were violets and snowdrops, hiding from the sun.

The back garden sloped down to four clay-soil garden beds and then on further to the rubbish heap where my father burned-off the garden cuttings every late Sunday afternoon - just like the other men on the North Shore who were also burning-off their garden waste. The sky became filled with a pall of smoke from Roseville to Wahroonga and the pungent aroma of burning gum leaves filled the air. The back fence was planted with "elephants" ears, a plant with big furry leaves. The house behind us had a chicken run with a rooster who cockadoodledo'd every morning to wake us up.

The weather had a profound effect on the plants, particularly during the extremely long droughts Australia suffered in the 1940s and mid-50s. Indeed, what modern-day people call Climate Change is nothing to what we experienced back in the 40s and 50s, and indeed, people long before us, back in the 1800s wrote poems about Climate Change, like John O'Brien's poem *Said Hanrahan* about a group of men pondering the drought and the likelihood of yet another flood coming after the drought. "'We'll all be rooned,' said Hanrahan as he chewed a piece of bark".

Thick red-brown dust from the inland droughts blew across the North Shore, leaving a sediment an inch thick on our furniture. Bushfires raged right up to the streets hugging the western side of the railway line where the pegs on my friend's mother's clothesline were singed after one close fire. Sometimes, water restrictions were imposed, partly because the Warragamba Dam hadn't started construction until the late 1940s.

An annual summer event was Ants' Day in our garden. For a couple of years we simply declared that we would not tread

28

on a single ant all day. Then I decided to actively help the ants by picking them up and carrying them to the other side of the very hot path. We even gave them ant food. But after a day of this I noticed that the ants didn't seem to want to cross over the path to the other side. They spent hours trailing back to where they had been when we picked them up. Nor did they seem to like the food we had provided. I finally cancelled Ants Day - apart from not treading on them. (Perhaps the big international Powers providing Aid could learn something from Ants Day.)

Our garden was a place where things came and went. One day when our washerwoman, Mrs Russell, brought her son Wayne with her, I joined him in one of the garden beds where we dug up a little brass machine that looked a bit like a clock. It had a handle, and once all the clay dirt was washed off it in the laundry, we found that it still worked and that it was a machine to tell the date. To this day, however, I do not know how it got there. I wasn't allowed to play with Wayne after that. He didn't speak properly, my mother said.

Our Roseville garden also yielded up a living treasure trove: its flowers. Every year at Christmastime my father would lean a small ladder against the Christmas bushes in the front garden and cut swathes of their blooms and put them in a bucket of water until one of his former New Guinea troops, now the driver of a double-decker bus, arrived at the bus stop outside our house, stopped the bus, to the great annoyance of the passengers, and came down to our front garden to pick up the Christmas bush bouquet for his family party.

However, more things tended to disappear rather than be found in our Roseville garden, including, I believed, my great-grandmother, Nan, who, by the time she lived with us, was a tiny 80+-year old with long white hair, but she had once been the red-headed belle of the Brisbane society balls.

When my parents came back from Nan's funeral, they informed three-year-old me that Nan had been buried. And when I looked at the gnarled and twisted branches of the old apricot tree halfway down our back garden, I knew where Nan must have been interred. My mother was hanging out the washing next morning, and I cried out: "There's Nan! Those branches are her hands, all twisted. She's holding out her hands!" My mother turned and glared at me. "Don't ever say such things again, Sandra!" she scolded, gathering up the dry sheets and towels into the clothes basket and fleeing back into the house.

The next thing to disappear in our garden was the little rag doll that my sister Steph and I shared, named Clementine. She was only about ten inches tall, but we loved her, and took her with us wherever we went. One day we left her sitting on the path near where my father was laying squares of new turf, while we went off to spray each other with the garden hose at the front of the house, for it was yet another hot day. But when we came back to pick up Clementine, she was nowhere to be seen. So began an intensive search, but to no avail.

We set up a missing-persons bureau on the back path, and tried to discover where Clementine might have gone. We worked out when she had last been seen, and retraced our movements that day. Could she have been abducted? Who might have taken her - the milkman? the clothes-prop man? the baker? But none of them, apart perhaps from the clothes-prop man, would have come down to the back garden - they all came to the tradesmen's door at the side of the house. We implored our father to dig up the turf he'd just laid. He obliged, but there was no sign of Clementine. Eventually we bowed to fate. Like in the song, our "darling Clementine" was "lost and gone forever".

Not long after Clementine disappeared, there was the incident of the two chocolate boxes which we had been given by a pair of old Theosophist ladies living at the Manor in Mosman where my father, as a GP, looked after them. Inside the chocolate boxes there were masses of the most glorious, pink-fluted glass beads in one box, and an equal number of black-jet beads in the other. We loved playing with those beads in the garden.

One day, however, we got a surprise. When we sat down in the garden and opened the boxes they were almost empty. Over the months, most of the beads had been lost in the garden.

The last thing that disappeared in our garden was a message in a bottle which we wrote when my father was concreting a new path. We signed the message "Sandra and Steph aged seven and five".

Perhaps one day a future archaeologist will dig up that bottle, along with a number of pink-fluted and black-jet beads and maybe a rag doll called Clementine, but no great-grandmother's bones.

CHAPTER 7

MEASLES AND WORMS

NORTH SHORE children were, and still are, subjected to all the best health care, and, dare I say, fads. When I was a child this included regular visits to the local Clinic near the bank at Roseville Station where we were weighed as infants on scales reminiscent of the weighing scales for flour at the local grocer's shop, and later, on proper old-style weighing machines. We had to swallow teaspoonfuls of a yellowish, creamy liquid called "emulsion", and quite early on, my father, being a doctor, insisted we take vitamin C (ascorbic acid) tablets. We cleaned our teeth at least twice daily with Ipana toothpaste, and my father coated our teeth from time-to--time with fluoride using a cottonwool swab. This was long before fluoride became fashionable.

North Shore children were infested with worms – as no doubt all children were back then. Worms were treated with Antepar, a syrupy drink. although, as I have already mentioned, one of my schoolfriends' mother made her drink gentian violet, which she then vomited purple all over the school pathway at morning tea time. But although worms were rampant on the North Shore, there was never a Tape Worm. Tape Worms were nasty things that happened on the other side of the Bridge, usually to boxing champions like Jimmy Carruthers.

Antibiotics were virtually non-existent in those days, though a primitive form of Penicillin did start to be used - my father took some and suffered a violent reaction to it and nearly died. Coughs were treated with Vicks Vapourub, and it was the done thing to have your tonsils and adenoids out when you were about seven or eight, an operation rarely done these days.

Of course, we all got the measles and German measles, mumps and chickenpox, but, thank goodness, very few North Shore children got Polio, or, as it was known in those days,

Infantile Paralysis. We were pretty terrified of getting it, but this didn't prevent us from playing hospital games where we made leg irons out of my mother's knitting needles and were wheeled around on a makeshift ambulance – my mother's traymobile. Some children got Diphtheria, which was probably the most serious disease that went around.

Being ill with a cold or a rash was often fun. We could listen to radio serials like Mrs 'Obbs and personalities such as Miss Anne Dryer on Kindergarten of the Air. and Bob Rogers' music programmes (after 78 years on air, Bob finally retired in 2021.)

When our baby teeth had fallen out and our adult teeth had replaced them we were taken to the Orthodontist where metal bands were fixed onto our protruding teeth for several years.

It wasn't until my father, after returning from the War, set up practice as a GP with a red light installed at our front gate. that I realised how ultra-healthy we North Shore people were. His patients sat on chairs along the front hall, and the front room was the surgery with its examination couch and screen and my father's university degree displayed on the wall. Most of his patients came with sore throats or fish bones stuck in their throats or tummy upsets and it wasn't until I came upon the publicity material which cascaded each morning through our letterbox from the drug companies that I realised just how fortunate we all were.

I loved the smell of those drug company brochures, all on shiny paper. Usually they had a cover showing the latest painting or sculpture by a world-famous modern artist, many of them practitioners of Swiss and German post-war, avant garde Art because most of the drug companies were Swiss. Seeing this art trained my eye to accept shapes and forms that I wasn't to learn about at school and only stumbled on years later in overseas galleries. But inside those glossy brochures was even more of an education in a grisly kind of way, for there, in explicit colour and gruesome detail, were pictures of some of the worst case-histories of horrendous skin complaints, gonorrhoea, palsy - you name it. I became inured to the sight of puss pouring from boils, rashes that had taken over people so totally you couldn't tell there was a person still there. I saw pictures of arms that were flippers and hands like hammers, eyes that were just holes, and heads that lolled. When I saw the works of Hieronymus Bosch later on there was nothing there to horrify me – I'd already seen worse. I doubt my father ever availed himself of any of the drugs advertised in these brochures - North Shore patients who had swallowed fishbones didn't need such medication.

My father kept a skeleton in his cupboard in his surgery. One day when my mother returned home from shopping, she came upon a curious scene. My young twin brother and sister, aged about 18 months, still wearing nappies, were sitting on the surgery floor, busily dismantling the skeleton, playing with a tibia here and a skull there. Meanwhile, our ironing lady, having fainted at the sight of the dismembered bones and then recovering by swigging at a bottle of whiskey she had also found in the cupboard, was ironing away merrily with a silly grin.

Later, my father decided to become an anaesthetist and the surgery was converted into my parents' bedroom. Sometimes at weekends my father experimented with the new anaesthetic drugs, injecting himself in the back garden and falling over backwoods onto the grass. He eventually became the senior honorary anaesthetist at Royal Prince Alfred Hospital and also gave anaesthetics at many other hospitals around Sydney.

Our days as a GP's household with a red light at the front gate ended when my father started working at Prince Alfred and the other hospitals, but he nevertheless continued to look after one or two local patients who continued to swallow fishbones and have tummy upsets.

CHAPTER 8

SENIOR SCHOOL

IT WAS ALMOST TIME to move on to Abbotsleigh's Senior or Upper School which was allegedly modelled on an English Public School. but our time in the Junior school was not quite over. We still had to enter, or in my case, endure, Remove. This was the year in which we were supposed to be inducted into the ways of the Upper School, a year in which to put away childish things and grapple with serious scholarship in the five years to come, leading up to the Leaving Certificate (later superseded by the Higher School Certificate after six years of study).

Remove A was the domain of Mrs Featherstone, whose resemblance to a dragon was unkind to dragons. I spent the greater part of my Remove year banished out onto the cold, windy and wet verandah for talking in class and other misdemeanours. When Mrs Featherstone occasionally deigned to allow me into the classroom, I observed that very little real education was occurring. Mrs Featherstone, who aped the Senior school teachers by wearing an academic gown - although she didn't appear to own to a degree - spent much of her time reading aloud to us from an endless novel about a group of friends who lived an uneventful existence on a houseboat in Sydney's Middle Harbour. I don't recall learning a single thing, academically, that entire Remove year. It was like being in limbo, like that no man's land between the two sides of the Berlin Wall where the searchlights scanned the territory mercilessly.

After the hell of Reomove, it was time to move on to Abbotsleigh's Senior or Upper School. (What I am about to report about the Senior School's standard of education is pre the arrival of the great revolutionary educationist, Betty Archdale, who pulled Abbotsleigh together and turned it into a school with an enviable academic reputation.)

Certainly, I found on my first day in the Senior School that it was a great change from the Junior School. All the teachers wore academic gowns, though I doubt that some of them, like Mrs Featherstone, had ever set foot in a university. Instead of always remaining in our designated classroom, as we had in the Junior School, we now tended to move like a herd of cattle from one classroom (or "form room" as they were called) to another depending on the subject. Foreign languages, or at least French, German and Latin, were introduced, and various levels of mathematics were imposed on us. I soon found my level in Maths: General, and at the lowest level of that. Nevertheless, I just managed to a achieve a Pass three years later in the Intermediate Certificate exam; the pass mark that year being 27 per cent.

Sport, too, became more formalised, with girls being sorted into hockey and basketball or tennis teams. For some odd reason, hockey was for the A Form and basketball was for the B form. The tennis teams were made up of the favourites of Mr Cody, the tennis coach - the only male teacher in the school at that time. Thus sorted, the teams were ready to do battle with opponents from PLC, Ravenswood or even Eastern Suburbs schools like SCEGGS Darlinghurst. But we didn't compete with teams from Catholic schools.

On our first day in the Upper school some of us were inducted into the Abbotsleigh Secret by a group of older girls. At Recess, they led us down to the Sewing Hut where they took us inside and pointed to a trapdoor in the floor with a ring in it for pulling it open. Silently, and very seriously, they pulled up the trapdoor to reveal a short flight of stairs leading to a tunnel. "That tunnel goes all the way to Barker," (the closest Anglican boys' school to Abbotsleigh), they explained in hushed tones. "And halfway along the tunnel are a whole lot of camp stretchers. It was in case of an air raid during the War."

Thus initiated, I went back to the classroom and started learning French, taught by a delightful woman called Mrs Fisher, whose first name was Malvina, meaning "bad wind", named after the islands where she had been born: the Maldives. Mrs Fisher invited anyone sufficiently interested in developing French conversational skills to join her in the quadrangle at lunchtime where we sat in the sun and spoke in hesitant French. Years later I found that although no Parisian could understand a word I uttered, the residents of Marseilles did.

General Maths was pretty disastrous from the start. We had a succession of teachers, starting with a woman who had spent most of her professional career working as a bus conductress. She was utterly incapable of controlling her classes. A dismal straggle of other General Maths teachers followed her, ending with the geography teacher who acted in a temporary capacity for the remainder of the term, resorting to agreeing each lesson to comply with our request for her to enunciate "a to the 125th", whereby she would start in her squeaky little voice: "Well girls "a to the 125th" means "a multiplied by a, multiplied by a, multiplied by a, …,".and she would continue on to the 125th after which the Recess bell would ring, thus ending the maths class for the day.

By contrast, our History classes were outstandingly interesting and stimulating. Our History teacher, Miss Hughesdon, nicknamed "Dot" because her name was Dorothy, was a superb teacher with the ability to enthuse even the dullest student.

Sadly, English was not taught with such brilliance. We plodded through our set texts and our teacher forced us to recite off by heart the punctuation in poems and even Shakespearean plays: "comma, comma, full stop, comma…" and so on. Not, I suspect, the ideal way to enjoy the Bard's words. One exception to this mutilation of the English language was Shakespeare Day. Each year we took a Shakespeare play to stage a scene from it, making the costumes and the scenery. One year we did two plays, *The Merchant of Venice* and *As You Like It*, and we made the scenery in my father's garage, with my mother bringing in pizzas to feed the starving team. My mother was much more interested in literature than most other girls' mothers, and she inspired her children to expand our vocabularies and to use new words in our essays instead of the humdrum cliches trotted out by most of our classmates.

Another non-academic highlight was raising money for the school swimming pool fund. I decided to cook and sell chocolate fudge cupcakes, stirring up a large saucepan of gooey chocolate on my mother's stove. By accident I tipped the saucepan over, blanketing the kitchen floor with melted chocolate. I couldn't waste it, so I scooped it up and put it back into the saucepan and the resulting cupcakes helped to swell the Swimming Pool Fund a little.

This success made me more ambitious and I compiled an Abbotsleigh Cookbook to sell. Unfortunately, this handsome volume was not proof-read by anyone and thus emerged from the printers titled *The Abbotsleigh Cookbook with Recipes by Mothers and Mistresses.* I wasn't old enough to recognise the *double entendre.*

Eventually, the swimming pool was constructed and opened in 1957, and we delighted in the unfamiliar sensation of swimming in a pool surrounded by gum trees rather than sea and sand. Unfortunately, the delights of the pool were somewhat marred by the painful plantar warts on our feet which many of us caught from the pool.

Our lunchtimes were spent lying in the clover on the Lower Oval, talking. Our friendships grew and some of the girls I nattered with on the Lower Oval are my friends to this day. But not all my lunch hours were spent so idyllically. I soon established a routine whereby I often spent lunchtime in detention supervised by the prefects on playground duty, picking up disgusting discarded pieces from other girls' lunches; orange peel, and tin foil from sweet packets that they had tucked away in nooks and crannies in the rockeries instead of doing the "right thing" and putting them in the bin. I got the Prefect Detentions for "being rude", ie, for not smarming up to them and pretending to have a crush on them like other girls did. Many

Thursday afternoons after school were also spent in Detention, writing out lines 700 times "I must not talk in -class". Many a Saturday morning, too, was spent travelling up by train to Abbotsleigh for even further detentions because there hadn't been sufficient hours left on Thursdays. On one occasion, however, I was wrongly accused of saying something loudly in Assembly, thus earning yet another detention. I complained to headmistress Miss Hirst, but she refused to remove my detention, saying: "You must learn to be a good Christian, Sandra, and accept punishment even if you didn't commit a crime. You must learn to turn the other cheek."

Sometimes in our lunchtimes we discussed serious subjects, such as whether or not we were snobbish. There was no doubt we were little snobs – at least in the eyes of those who lived outside the purlieus of Roseville to Wahroonga. North Shore snobbery was imbibed like mother's milk: we seemed just naturally to hold certain opinions and beliefs. For example, it was regarded as vulgar to have pierced ears or to eat meat pies in public or to have a tattoo. We had our own occupational pecking order too, based on the simple questions: a) Would you like to live next door to a. ....? and b) Would you like to marry a. ....? The first question evinced a long list of modes of behaviour in potential neighbours, such as: we wouldn't want to live next door to people wearing just singlets without a shirt; people who parked their cars on their front lawn; motorbike owners in general; funny foreign cooking smells; a trail of male visitors in the afternoon (this must have been a prejudice of my mother's). But the things that clinched our answers boiled down to the occupation of the head of the neighbouring household. We dreaded the thought of an undertaker living next door. A clergyman (Protestant of course) would be just tolerable, but we suspected he'd let his lawn grow long and his fence would keel over. A chiropractor was beyond the pale, as was a jockey, or a photographer. As to the question "Would you marry a. ...?" The thought of marrying a butcher struck fear into us, almost as repellent as the thought of marrying a hairdresser.

Yes, the North Shore was squeamish and precious but part of this came from the predominantly English background of many of the people who had settled on the North Shore in its early days. Moreover, although North Shore people, along with those from the Eastern Suburbs, tended to have two cars and a dishwasher first, the rest of Sydney soon caught up as the country became more affluent, and thus some of the snobbish tastes and prejudices filtered through to the rest of the suburbs. Nevertheless, a lot of non-North Shore people went on using zinc cream and had tattoos.

CHAPTER 9

THE BUSH BROTHERS AND
THE SCRUB SISTERS

THE EVANGELICAL WING of the Church of England was beginning to wield its scythe through the North Shore during the 1950s. Those who were High Church were snubbed by the Low Church clergy who dubbed them "pseudo-Catholics". Meanwhile, the other Protestant religions pottered along quietly.

Religion didn't impinge on me much until I went to Abbotsleigh. I suppose our family was agnostic, despite my great-uncle Wal having been an Anglican archdeacon until he was defrocked for marrying his wife's sister after his wife had died. He was, however, re-frocked after a time because his ability to raise money for the Church was indispensable.

My mother's side of the family, too, had been very religious. My grandfather was a Theosophist and had run off to Kathmandu with a lady Theosophist, leaving my grandmother to bring up five children alone. The day he left, my mother, aged 12,, brought up as a vegetarian, went down to the local butcher and bought some chops which she cooked and served up to her three sisters and brother.

So, as children, we were not sent off to Sunday School by parents wanting a bit of peace and quiet on Sunday mornings. On the other hand, our good friend, Bruce, from down the street, did attend Sunday School and would return looking smug and chanting "I'm H-A-P-P-Y. I HOPE I AM…I'M SURE I AM… I'M H-A-P-P-Y". Bruce tried to get us to join him at Sunday school, but we preferred to go to the beach.

The Evangelical wing of the Church of England was beginning to nose through Abbotsleigh - like all the private Anglican schools in Sydney, despite our Headmistress, Miss Hirst, being High Church and crossing herself – much to the annoyance of a group of proselytising evangelical parents who were working hard to get rid of her.

We sang hymns in Assembly each morning, and many of my classmates went to Communion and belonged to the Crusaders. They also trooped off to the city to hear Billy Graham when he came to Sydney to proselytise. Some of my classmates came back from Billy Graham starry-eyed, grasping photographs of him which they kissed from time-to-time before tucking the photo into their Bible. We had the Rev Begbie once a week preaching at assembly, Canon Payne also came regularly. Around Easter, we had the annual visit of the Bush Brothers, alternating with the Scrub Sisters, who described their evangelical work to help the poverty-stricken children in the Outback, and left us all with little cardboard Lent boxes into which we were to put our pennies and threepences as penance for Easter, after which an official came and collected the boxes and tipped our coins into the Church's coffers. The Bush Brothers' and Scrub Sisters' annual talks – held in the school gym-cum-assembly room - went on for a long time and were so boring that one year I decided to nudge and lean against the girl sitting next to me on the gym floor, causing her to lean against the next girl, and so on down the row, until the last girl was knocked completely sideways. This activity was noticed by the teachers who were sitting on the dais with the speaker, and I was excluded from future Bush Brother/Scrub Sister talks and banished to the Art Room the following year, where I was surprised to find a group of other girls - all the old familiar denizens of the Detention Room – and some of the teachers, who were smoking and telling jokes.

Later, when I was 14, the evangelical tenor of the school went up a notch or two with the arrival of Deaconess Nelson, who held Divinity classes twice a week. We didn't learn anything in these classes about great religious art or music. Instead, our Divinity lessons consisted of little else than having to cut out pictures of the Disciples from miniature Scripture picture books and sticking them into our exercise books. However, the

Deaconess once asked us to write an essay on a selection of topics. I chose Noah's Ark. We had to write nine pages on our topic so I asked my father what he thought an ark would have looked like in the olden days. He checked out the Bible and found that it measured 21 cubits long. He then concluded that it must have been a flat raft, probably made of logs tied together - a far cry from the arks in the picture books with little pointed red tiled roofs. So I drew some diagrams and wrote a page or two about the Ark. Then I added the names of some of the animals I thought would have sailed on the ark. I managed to fill three more pages with this list, but then I ran out of animals until I thought maybe Australian kangaroos and kookaburras and emus and wallabies would have gone too. Having thus filled the requisite nine pages, I handed in my essay to the Deaconess. She returned it marked in red ink. The first three pages had 9/10 on them and the comment: "Excellent". The rest of the essay had 3/10 and the comment: "Only the African animals entered the Ark."

Religion impinged again on Speech Day when' each year,' Archbishop Howard Mowll, the Anglican Primate of Sydney, officiated at the annual prize-giving in the marquee erected for the occasion on the Upper Oval. We were always fascinated by the Archbishop as we had heard a rumour that his private parts had been chopped off by terrorists when he was stationed as a missionary in China. One Speech Day it was so windy the marquee started to flap alarmingly and suddenly the guy ropes holding it down began to snap. The parents fled from the marquee, leaving Archbishop Mowll bravely defending his manhood by holding on to a guy rope with all his mighty weight, thus managing to keep the marquee from flying away. His cassock, however, despite billowing, did not manage to reveal anything untoward or missing to our prying eyes.

Archbishop Mowll, who was a kindly fellow, shook hands with me at several Speech days when I climbed past the buckets of hydrangeas and Christmas bush onto the dais in the marquee where he handed out the prizes. Before each Speech Day, I and other prize-winners were called in to the

Headmistress's study to be told that we must not feel that we were superior to the rest of our classmates because "The real aim of Abbotsleigh is to bring up good wives and mothers."

Above all, my deepest regret about the religious teaching at Abbotsleigh was its third-rate quality. We never heard about great religious art, inspired religious writing - such as the English in the King James version of the Bible. We never heard any magnificent religious music, apart from the hymns we sang at assembly, drummed out on an old piano. Indeed, we never heard of the great moments in the history of religion. All we got was boring monologues of Low Church doctrine.

CHAPTER 10

LET OUT OF SCHOOL

THE SCHOOL HOLIDAYS for the North Shore meant Going Away – but only somewhere in Australia in those days (except for one girl who went overseas on a cruise to India during one of the school holidays). Going Away meant that sometimes we even learnt a bit about How the Other Half Lived, but mostly everyone went to the usual smart resorts. For the May, winter, holidays, the more fashionable of my schoolfriends, garbed in their twinsets and tartan skirts, went with their parents up to the Hydro in the Blue Mountains at Medlow Bath. What they did there while their parents sat in the bar or went off to play golf and sit in the bar at the Blackheath Golf Club, I do not know – my schoolmates came back from their time at the Hydro giggling and passing knowing looks between them, but there was no mention of bush walks or sausages grilled over an open fire.

My family, on the other hand, went to Faulconbridge (a few townships lower down the Mountains from Medlow Bath), where my grandparents had retired and built a house on a sizeable property with a small orchard, a paddock, a cave, and a large pond with sand in the middle on which I and my sister, sat and played "islands". Our grandparents had planted an orchard full of fruit trees, built rockeries, made ponds, and created a paradise for two small children - me and Steph. Each day began with Grandad making cups of tea and listening to the ABC news on his tall radio which sat on the windowsill looking out over the mountains and gullies to Mt Kurrajong. Then we sat down to a table covered with a blue checked cloth and had hot porridge, before running out into the paddock to make potato men, or going down to the big rock which had a cave underneath it. The currawongs called "See ya later" to each other as they swooped through the gum trees, while my grandparents wheeled their barrows up and down the vegetable patches. My grandmother, whom we called by her first name, Isabel, took a load of freshly-picked vegetables down to the markets at Springwood once a week where she sold them to a stall holder. She refused to keep chooks, however, saying they were dirty, and she relied on getting her eggs from old Mrs Stratton down the road.

Steph and I spent a lot of time in the big pond, sitting on a sand island in the middle, making little villages out of the sand. Sometimes when it was a warm day we'd just sit in the long grass in another paddock with the sun beating down and the wasps buzzing and butterflies darting over our heads.

Lunchtime began when we heard Isabel calling out Grandad's name: "Arthur!" and we all went into the kitchen where Isabel had been cooking a roast on her fuel stove. Lunch in the next room, was the big meal of the day: roast lamb or chicken, apple sauce, gravy, crisp baked potatoes, followed by apple pie and custard; Isabel was a great country cook. Then a quiet time on the verandah, listening to the blowflies banging against the fly-screen wire, before tumbling out again for a walk along the track leading to the man who lived in an old double-decker bus in the bush with his pet kangaroo which we were allowed to feed with biscuits.

Coming back, we'd pass Mrs Jocelyn's little fibro cottage with its Cooper-louvered front verandah. Mrs Jocelyn had very primitive false teeth with bright orange gums. Steph one day stuck a slice of orange into her mouth and strutted about, saying "I'm Mrs Jocelyn." To punish her, Isabel locked Steph into the pantry for an hour. But it was not really a punishment - we loved being cooped up in the pantry among the tantalising smells and the jars of preserved fruit, biscuits, and jams.

We sometimes sat in the garden across the road with old Mrs Dight who lived in a tiny fibro cottage where she cooked on a methylated spirits stove because she had no electricity installed, and we listened to her read *Alice in Wonderland* to us. She had a gold bangle which she allowed me to wear while we sat in her garden beside the sun dial and she read to us. We also heard *Alice*

Through the Looking Glass one winter holiday. We also spent some time sitting above the cave halfway down our grandparents' property with the daughter of the local corner store who had a wooden leg. One year, she had a friend staying who lived on Cockatoo Island in Sydney Harbour because her father was in the Navy. She sang songs like "Cigarettes and Whiskey and Wild Wild Wimmen" until my grandmother banished her, telling us she wasn't the right sort of girl for us to be playing with.

In the evening, after a supper around the fireplace where we cooked toast over the fire on long pronged forks, we had hot baths and then went to bed under huge eiderdowns, listening to the creaking and popping of the corrugated iron roof as it adapted to the cold mountain night air. We heard Grandad going up to the front gate to hang the milk billy-cans ready for the milkman to come past next day on his horse. And we listened for the sound of the toot of the last railway engine as the Fish or the Chips ended its day's toil.

Occasionally Isabel sent us outside to play all day because her former schoolfriends from MLC Croydon were coming up on the train for the day. (She was strictly Anglican, with a brother who was an Anglican archdeacon, but there apparently wasn't a suitable Anglican school near Strathfield where she grew up). She had prepared a special feast for her old classmates on her fuel stove and they dined in the drawing room among my grandmother's collection of porcelain, and, amid much giggling, pulled up their skirts and showed off their suspenders to each other.

One day, a big storm was threatening as we raced back down the bumpy road to the house. Lightning zig-zagged down and thunder rolled out of the black clouds. Isabel and Grandad were standing in the driveway waiting for us and I raced up and said "That thunder is electricity in the clouds." Isabel looked at me and said: "No, it's the clouds knocking their heads together." I replied, "It's electricity, isn't it, Grandad?" Grandad looked at me and hesitated, then he put his arm around Isabel and said "It's the clouds knocking their heads together."

He was a very kind man.

We led a completely free existence at Faulconbridge, but even back home in Roseville the freedom we had as children is in stark contrast to today's children's restricted activities where often they aren't even expected to catch the bus to school and instead are driven to school by their mothers. The local bush up at East Lindfield was free for us to roam in and to pick wild-flowers unpoliced. We rode our bikes without helmets, and when we went out on family trips to the bush further afield, we lit fires and cooked sausages and chops, unrestricted by fire bans. We did, however, always carefully put out the fire before we went home.

We also had completely unregulated annual fireworks nights which normally went off happily. One year, however, our fireworks night was a disaster. Our dentist had invited us to his home at Killara for the fireworks and we had purchased our Chrysanthemum Fountains, Catherine Wheels, Roman Candles and sparklers with anticipation, and packed them in bags. When we arrived at our dentist's house, the fire was already crackling in the back garden while the parents were drinking cocktails in the house. We settled down beside the fire in anticipation of a long and enjoyable evening as the other young guests had brought equally large bagfuls. But, to our horror, our dentist host picked up all the bags and emptied their contents onto the fire. in one go . An ear-shattering explosion erupted into the Killara night and we fled to safety. That was the end of our fireworks night - it cast a pall over the rest of that winter.

But summer was on the way. The North Shore Summer holidays were spent at the beach – the Northern Beaches of course, although some girls went up to the Central Coast. Garbed in our bubble bathing suits – my mother wouldn't let us wear Speedos, which she said were "common" -- and carrying our inflatable Surfoplanes, beach towels and foldable headrests, our noses untouched by white zinc cream which my mother also thought was "common" (we treated sunburn with cold tea. In those days our skin always peeled, but later on, for some odd

48

reason, it didn't). We started going to Collaroy and Narrabeen but then we found Bilgola farther north which at that time had only one house, a mysterious bungalow with wide verandas, surrounded by palm trees, tucked away in the jungle behind the beach.

Driving back home each Sunday after the beach, we'd stop off at Brysons' fish shop at Narrabeen Lakes and buy fish-and-chips wrapped in newspaper which we devoured in the back seat. Later on, we ventured up to Avoca on the Central Coast and stayed in a cottage on the point belonging to a friend of my father's. Later, too, when we were older, we joined the sailing club at Clareville on Pittwater where we sailed VJs and met boys from Shore and Barker. Very occasionally, we ventured up as far as Palm Beach, the privileged stamping ground of both the North Shore and the Eastern Suburbs wealthier denizens. Quite often, too, we went to Long Reef where my father liked to fish off the rocks and we would go and swim in The Basin, a natural rock pool ideal for the kids from the country who came down to stay and to learn to swim there.

Back home for the rest of the holidays was also where we learned the really important things that were passed down in the age-old way from the older kids to the younger ones, and sometimes even from our parents. We learned how to get hold of silkworm eggs laid on blotting paper by the silkworms owned by the school form ahead of us who sold them to us. Our experiments with different types of leaves proved that mulberry leaves were superior to lettuce, hydrangea, or violet leaves. Soon we had cartons of fat silkworms chewing away on mulberry leaves and we began to run out of leaf supplies. Mrs Dot Morris from across the road had a mulberry tree in her back garden, so we asked if we might have a few leaves. Within days, to her vented horror, her tree was stripped bare. Spinning the silk from the cocoons was one of the skills we picked up, letting the cocoon bob about in a glass of warm water while we wound the silk into a skein on a piece of cardboard. Watching the silkworm moths mate with their eerily sexy pulsation after breaking out of the cocoons was also an education not to be found in the classroom. We also learned the age-old skipping chants, how to play jacks, cats' cradles, and hopscotch, Snakes and Ladders, Ludo, Monopoly and Strip Jack Naked. Often, as the summer holidays dragged on and on and we got bored, our mother, to her great credit, inspired us to draw islands and place roads and farms and villages on them and populate them with little communities.

Outdoors we loved Statues and O'Grady Says, but the Wedding was our favourite. In the hall cupboard, after the War ended, my father had stored in it a brown leather greatcoat, a Japanese gas mask, a silk parachute, and a very sharp Japanese ceremonial sword with a bit of cloth tied to its handle with some Japanese writing on it. We weren't allowed to touch the sword because it was so sharp. From time-to-time my father got the sword out and oiled it carefully. (Later on, he found out how to send it back to the Japanese officer who had owned it. The officer, who had become a Buddhist monk, replied, thanking my father and sending a wall scroll.) What interested us most was the parachute which we took out of the hall cupboard and spread over the grass in the back garden, its silk billowing. Then we'd take it in turns to dress up as brides in it, creating a bridal train that would rival that of any royal wedding.

We often sat on our front verandah balustrade with our friend Bruce and patiently waited for the occasional car to pass by on what was later to become a very busy road as cars became more available. We learned how to tell a Pontiac from a Studebaker, a Ford from an Austin, but there were no Holdens in Roseville. We ourselves started with an Austin during the War and then got first, a Morris Oxford, and then also a Fiat. Having two cars was rare in those early days, but my father needed an extra one because he was a doctor. (As time moved on, more and more North Shore families had two cars – or more.)

Listening to the radio was a favourite pastime. Steph and I also used to rush home from school to listen to Biggles. This on-going radio saga became bogged down finally when Biggles and Bertie got stuck down a sewer. Week-after-week, their dilemma dragged on: "Is that you Biggles?" Gurgle, gurgle, gurgle. "Is that you Bertie?" Gurgle, gurgle, gurgle. In the end we switched off Biggles, leaving him down the sewer forever.

Our parents sometimes took us to the theatre. This was something few of our friends did and I'm very grateful that my parents thought it important to see visiting stars like Katherine Hepburn and Robert Helpmann in the "Taming of the Shrew" and the "Merchant of Venice", and Margot Fonteyn and Rudolf Nureyev dancing. We also saw musicals like "South Pacific", "Oklahoma", and "Brigadoon" and were taken to Christmas pantomimes. A great event was the visiting Chinese Opera which we saw on two occasions, inspiring us to re-enact the dramatic music and dancing, using pots and pans from the kitchen as makeshift percussion instruments.

We also went to Roseville Baths on weekdays when the tide was high enough so that the water was cleaner. The old Baths, located in the midst of a mangrove swamp close to the old Roseville Bridge, were the haunt of local boys who rampaged over the baths, jumping and diving off the diving board and harassing the public-school girls in their Speedos who nevertheless hung on to the boys' every antic. The babies' pool first thing on a summer's morning when nobody else was there, could be very beautiful. Red gum leaves floated in the clear water at high tide and we had the Baths to ourselves. Nevertheless, the Baths were totally unhygienic and were the source of much of the local GPs' incomes from the nasal and throat infections that were endemic to the North Shore.

CHAPTER 11

THE NORTH SHORE MATING GAME

BEFORE I EMBARK ON the mating habits of the North Shore, I need to explain that what I will describe occurred in the late 1950's - before the introduction of The Pill. That contraceptive miracle, which was to break on to our world only a few years later, was to radically change the teenage mating game around the world, and what I will now relate will look extraordinarily quaint and old-fashioned to any member of the post-Pill generations. Nevertheless, I think it's worth documenting.

When we reached Third year, it was time to attend Dancing Class. Some of the mothers who had older daughters at Abbotsleigh contacted my mother and inducted her into the ritual of sending us to Miss Kay's Dancing Class in the Marion Street Hall in Killara. Only boys from the North Shore private Protestant schools – Barker and Knox - as well as Shore and Grammar (even though they were situated outside the North Shore) and girls from Abbotsleigh, PLC and Ravenswood, were permitted to attend Miss Kay's, and the boys were to be one or two years older than the girls, who were 14 or 15. Talk about a Rite of Passage.

The mothers organised a carpool of fathers who were to pick up the girls each Thursday evening to take us to Miss Kay's. We wore our first pair of high heels with dresses or blouses and hooped skirts. We were permitted to wear a little bit of lipstick. The boys, garbed in their school uniforms, arrived at the hall in their fathers' second cars as they were now the holders of a driver's licence (which in those days started at age 17). Outside the Marion Street Hall, Killara, older boys lounged around, assessing the new batch of girls and throwing the occasional double-bunger firework under the foundations of the hall.

Inside was a large room with polished floorboards and a stage with a piano. The girls were to sit on one side of the room, the boys on the other. Then the Misses Kay sisters entered the stage. On our first evening at Dancing Class one Miss Kay sat down at the piano, while her sister, dressed in a leopard skin skirt and black stockings, clapped her hands and announced that we would start with The Quickstep. She then demonstrated the dance steps to her petrified audience. Next, she clapped her hands again and told the boys to take their partners. As we girls sat in terror, a vast wave of boys came rushing and sliding over the polished floor towards us. Boys grabbed girls, yanking them out of their seats onto the dance floor as the other Miss Kay started playing the piano. After the Foxtrot, we did the Canadian Three-step, or was it Two-step? It didn't matter – the way we danced mangled the protocol anyway, and then the Waltz. Gradually as the weeks went by we began to talk to the boys who had yanked us onto the dance floor. I soon discovered the best topic of conversation with a boy was to ask him about his car - or, to be more exact, his father's car. He would then regale me with an endless spiel about the carburetor or the crankshaft until the piano stopped and we were able to return to our seats.

In Term Two we began to feel more confident, and when some of the boys announced that we should demand to be allowed to do Rock 'n Roll we girls readily agreed. However, the Misses Kay refused to allow such common music and gyrations until we all went on strike and refused to get up on to the dance floor until R 'n Roll was allowed. Finally, a compromise was reached and the evening was split half-and-half traditional ballroom dancing and half Rock 'n Roll. We had all been born a couple of years earlier than the start of the Baby Boomer generation, but I have often felt we were premature Baby Boomers because our teenage, and subsequent activities put us unequivocally into that demographic - for better or worse.

The mothers, meanwhile, were telephoning each other, making lists of the girls and boys they felt were acceptable to invite to dances in their homes. My best friend's mother organised a big dance at their house in Lindfield which had a curved room with a dance floor. My friend and I were madly enamoured of a tall blond hunk of a boy called Howard, and we were desperate to get him invited. Somehow my friend's mother got hold of his address, and an invitation was duly sent off. On the night of the dance we stood tremulously at the top of the steps, greeting our guests alongside my friend's mother, the hostess, and waited breathlessly for Howard to arrive. But there was no sign of him. We were downcast - he had snubbed us! Finally, a very thin boy wearing glasses and pimples came up the stairs. "I'm Howard H," he announced. We had got the wrong name! The blond Adonis we had been expecting was not called Howard H at all.

As time went on, the mothers tactfully retired from the parties, leaving us to get on with things. My best friend had inducted me into the intricacies of the North Shore Code which she had learned from her older sister. Holding hands was Number 1 on the Code. Number 2 was kissing, and so it progressed from then on, in even numbers, up to 8. All these stages were "Above the waist". From 8 onwards it was "Below the waist" in incremental stages until 14, which marked "doing IT". The Code was carried out at the pictures or, better still, at the drive-in, or at a party when the lights were turned down and the music turned on to Buddy Holly and the kissing began. The Code continued later in the boy's car on the way home

As far as I know, nobody in our Form ever went to 14, but some of the girls in the lower form did, or at least alleged they did. We called them "the Types" They would turn up at school on Monday mornings wearing remnants of make-up, and the occasional earring still left on. Most of them left school after the Intermediate. I did get to know some of the girls in the lower Form and some of them were very nice. I got to know them because I was allowed to do Art and Craft, having shown no talent for Latin. A couple of those girls turned out to be extremely successful in later years, running businesses and art galleries etc.

And so we started going out with the North Shore boys. Some of them I know to this day. Some of them married girls I went to school with. Many of them, I'm afraid to say, were not particularly bright, but all of them managed to get good jobs in big firms if they didn't have the brains to go to university - their family connections paid off. I, meanwhile, decided the following year to widen my pool of friends by attending Miss Mann's dancing class at Lindfield, which the State school North Sydney High boys attended. I soon got to know them and found them infinitely more interesting than the private school boys, and soon I was attending parties in their homes too. They were more "with it" than the Shore, Barker and Knox boys, wearing suede shoes and listening to Dave Brubeck records.

We went to the Regatta each year, wearing smart outfits along with our school hats, and barracked for Shore, it being the only GPS school we knew. We also started dating boys we had met at dancing class, some of whom were somewhat raw behind the ears, while others, like X, who would pick me up in his father's Jag, had learned a thing or two. One day, X and I were sitting at the top of Long Reef in the Jag, admiring the view, when I heard the sound of pebbles and stones rattling down the cliff face. Peering out through the windscreen, I suddenly saw a head appear over the top of the cliff. Strangely, the head was not facing the cliff face as its owner climbed up the cliff, but was facing out to sea. Eventually, the owner of the head emerged, staggering backwards over the top of the cliff. It was B, a boy who had taken a shine to me, whom, I had believed I had politely discarded. The last time I had gone out with him he took me to the car races at Bathurst. It had been a cold, rainy morning, and as the rain worsened most of the races were called off, and my escort suggested we go back via the Blue Mountains where some of his North Shore schoolmates had been attending a Scouts weekend at the Blue Mountains grammar school. Thus, we drove down the Highway to through the school gates where we searched the grounds for his school's Scout camp. Alas, all we saw were a couple of abandoned collapsed tents lying among their tent pegs in the rain. We then went into the main schoolhouse where we found 20 or so boys sitting forlornly around an empty table in the school dining room.

"Have you brought us some food?" they asked expectantly. "All we have is some sausages we had planned to fry over an open fire."

Realising that time was ticking by and nobody was going to do anything about lunch, I found a large frying pan in the adjacent kitchen and started cooking their sausages, along with some toasted buns. This was all devoured with no thanks, and I finally persuaded B to take me home. It would be the last time I saw B, I thought thankfully. But no, there he was, climbing backwards up the cliff at Long Reef.

"We climb backwards as a bit of a challenge," B explained to me as he walked past us sitting in X's Jaguar. I thanked my lucky stars I no longer counted him among my acquaitances.

However, I was to come across B one more time. I happened to be walking home along the footpath in Archbold Road, Roseville, one afternoon, when I heard a screech of brakes as a car turned out of a side street into Archbold Road. As it turned, the front passenger door of the car flew open, and a woman rolled out onto the road. The car stopped abruptly, and the driver got out and rushed to the other side of the car where the woman lay on the road. As he pulled her to her feet and brushed her down, I realised he was none other than B. As I watched, unrecognised, from the footpath, he guided the woman back into the car and drove off. I was later to learn that the woman who had fallen out of his car was his older sister, the headmistress of a well-known girls' school.

CHAPTER 12

FAREWELL NORTH SHORE

BY THE TIME I was to do the Intermediate Certificate my mother had become thoroughly tired of Abbotsleigh. She felt the standard of teaching was too low - which it was on the whole - and after the Intermediate my parents decided to uproot me and my two sisters, Steph and Ingrid, from Abbotsleigh and send us to Roseville Girls' College, at that time quite a small establishment (it was later to drop the word "Girls" from its name). In retrospect. I think there was nothing intrinsically wrong with Abbotsleigh. It did what it set out to do in those days: produce good wives and mothers. My problem was that I simply didn't fit in or conform to those aims.

Abbotsleigh, to its credit, was on the verge of appointing Betty Archdale as Headmistress. But my mother's letter announcing our resignations arrived before the announcement of Miss Archdale's appointment, and, despite the entreaties of my French teacher, Mrs Fisher, begging my mother to let us stay at Abbotsleigh, my mother, who had been getting itchy feet about the North Shore, decided that she'd had enough of Abbotsleigh. Roseville Girls College it was to be. I found myself in a class of only six other girls on my arrival there. and I almost wished I was back at Abbotsleigh. Sadly, the standard of teaching at this little establishment in Roseville was even lower than at Abbotsleigh in those days, although it, too, has pulled up its socks in recent years.

The final straw came when the art teacher threw my paint water over a picture I was painting, saying "That makes it look much better", and I decided then and there to leave Roseville Girls College and enrol at the Julian Ashton Art School, an establishment I'd heard about from my grandfather, who had studied there many years earlier. So I went home and found the

Art School telephone number in the phone book and rang it. An old man's voice answered. I asked whether I could enrol.

"How old are you"?" asked the voice.

"I'm 16," I replied.

"Well that's old enough for Julian Ashtons. Where do you live?" he asked.

"Roseville," I replied.

"Just take the bus to Wynyard and then walk up North George Street to the old Mining Museum near the Harbour Bridge," he said.

It turned out that the "voice" belonged to Henry Gibbons, the white-bearded doyen of the School.

I told my father that evening that I had decided to leave school and go to Julian Ashtons. With typical lenience, he didn't baulk at this, saying: "I'll ring the art school in the morning and get you enrolled." I told him I'd already enrolled, and he didn't demur. He knew how keen I was on art, and how I'd been having lessons in watercolours from Grandad since I was 12. He and I and Grandad often went into town at weekends to paint in Hyde Park or in the inner suburbs.

A day or so later, I spent my last day at Roseville Girls' College. I packed my books and put them in my bike basket along with my gym tunic. I threw my sandshoes into their bag and hung it on the handlebars of my bike. Then, with the whole school leaning out the windows and waving and cheering me goodbye, I mounted my bike and set off. Suddenly, my sand-shoe bag, hanging on the handlebar, got stuck in the front wheel and the bike shuddered to a halt, then the back wheel came up head-over-heels throwing me to the ground. A less dignified exit could hardly be imagined.

The moment I walked up George Street the next day and entered the Julian Ashton Art School a big, wide, wonderful world opened for me. Thus, my schooling on the North Shore came to an end (although I did finish my secondary education, catching up two years in one at a coaching college, and then went on to university). Shortly after I joined the Art School, we moved to Clifton Gardens, Mosman – Northside, but not North Shore, and thus my life on the North Shore came to an end.

I had taken my first. tentative flight from a friendly, comfortable, self-satisfied nest, out into the big wide world, a nest which, despite its elitism and stodginess, had provided me with a stable, safe start in life. But it was wonderful to fly the coop, and I never suffered another Detention for talking, or speaking my mind. Indeed, I was later to earn my living by those very things.

SOME OTHER BOOKS BY THIS AUTHOR

All Titles are available as e-books and Print-on-Demand (POD) worldwide.

OTTOLINE: THE LIFE OF LADY OTTOLINE MORRELL (Chatto & Windus UK); Coward McCann & Geoghegan (USA) 1975-76

POWER FOR THE PEOPLE (Svengali Press Aust., UK. USA) 2015

GARSINGTON REVISITED (Svengali Press, Aust., UK, USA) 2017

AFTER THE ULTIMATE VIRUS (Svengali Press Aust, UK. USA) 2020

The Svengali Press publishes good books which the big publishers overlook. Our list can be viewed at: www.svengalipress.com.au

If you have an unpublished manuscript ready for publication, please contact us for assessment at: sjd@cybersydney.com.au

Printed in Australia
AUHW010830080322
360601AU00004B/4

9 781922 698414